THE EVERYTHING KIDS' CONNECT THE DOTS

PUZZLE AND ACTIVITY BOOK

Fun is as easy as 1-2-3 with these cool
and crazy follow-the-numbers puzzles

Scot Ritchie

D1473182

Adamsmedia

avon, massachusetts

DIRECTOR OF INNOVATION Paula Munier

EDITORIAL DIRECTOR Laura M. Daly

EXECUTIVE EDITOR, SERIES BOOKS Brielle K. Matson

ASSOCIATE COPY CHIEF Sheila Zwiebel

ACQUISITIONS EDITORS Kerry Smith & Katie McDonough

PRODUCTION EDITOR Casey Ebert

An Everything® Series Book.
Everything® and everything.com® are registered trademarks of F+W Media, Inc.

Published by Adams Media, a division of F+W Media, Inc.
57 Littlefield Street, Avon, MA 02322. U.S.A.
www.adamsmedia.com

ISBN-10: 1-59869-647-5
ISBN-13: 978-1-59869-647-9

Printed by RR Donnelley, Harrisonburg, VA, USA.

December 2015

10   9

This publication is designed to provide accurate and authoritative information with regard to the subject matter covered. It is sold with the understanding that the publisher is not engaged in rendering legal, accounting, or other professional advice. If legal advice or other expert assistance is required, the services of a competent professional person should be sought.
—From a *Declaration of Principles* jointly adopted by a Committee of the American Bar Association and a Committee of Publishers and Associations

Many of the designations used by manufacturers and sellers to distinguish their products are claimed as trademarks. When those designations appear in this book and Adams Media was aware of a trademark claim, the designations have been printed with initial capital letters.

Cover illustrations by Dana Regan.
Interior illustrations by Kurt Dolber.
Puzzles by Scot Ritchie.

This book is available at quantity discounts for bulk purchases.
For information, please call 1-800-289-0963.

CONTENTS

INTRODUCTION

It's easy to imagine that the first game of connect the dots was played by somebody sitting by the fire staring up at the night sky. There are billions of dots waiting to be connected. Maybe they even took a stick from the fire and made the first pencil, joining together pebbles on the ground. It's amazing what you can create just by stringing things together. The good news is that since that ancient fireside episode, numbers have been invented and now it's a lot easier!

In *The Everything® Kids' Connect the Dots Puzzle and Activity Book*, we've gathered together subjects from our most popular books. Do you like sports, dinosaurs, insects, or princesses? There's something for everybody. We've created more than 100 brand new puzzles with games, interesting facts, and trivia. You can draw everything from a flying dinosaur (even though dinosaurs never flew) to a laughing shark (and sharks don't laugh—at least as far as we know).

The rules for playing connect the dots are simple. If you can count, you can play. Just get out your pencils or crayons and follow the numbers. Sometimes there are letters instead of numbers, so you follow your ABCs to create a picture. As an extra bonus, *The Everything® Kids' Connect the Dots Puzzle and Activity Book* is a coloring book, too; once you reveal the secret image on each page, you can color it in.

If you already know how to draw, this book will give you confidence to go further and try new things. It's exciting to see an elephant or racecar emerge from the page just by connecting numbers.

If you're just learning to draw, these puzzles will show you how simple it can be. Anyone can do it. *The Everything® Kids' Connect the Dots Puzzle and Activity Book* isn't going to make you a Picasso overnight, but when you think about it, maybe if he had been given a copy he might have been famous when he was a lot younger. Too bad Michelangelo didn't have one for the Sistine Chapel—it would have made it a lot easier.

To make things even more interesting, we've added challenges when you least expect them, so make sure you keep your wits about you.

We've jammed tons of weird and interesting facts inside, too—who said you can't have fun while you're learning! Did you know there's an ant in South America whose bite is so speedy he holds the world record for the fastest movement by any living thing? Chomp! Did you hear about the basketball player in Florida who set the record for spinning the most balls at one time? How many do you think that is: 6, 10, 15? I'm not telling, but if you check out Chapter 1, puzzle 10 you can see for yourself. Did you know that in the first lacrosse games (played by Native Americans), the number of players could be in the thousands and the field could be many miles long?

So if you're ready, let's get started. Grab your pencil or crayon (but definitely no burning sticks from the fire) and let's go connect the dots!

Chapter 1

SPORTS AND GAMES

Kickin' It!

Kickball is an all-American game invented in 1942 by U.S. soldiers stationed in North Africa. Now it's played all over the United States. It looks like somebody who's not part of the team has joined the game. Can you figure out who it is?

Why can't Cinderella
play Kickball?

— · — · · — · · —

Because she keeps
running away from the ball!

Roger Dodger

Dodgeball is played around the world in organized leagues or just when friends get together. You have to be very fast if you don't want to get hit. Somebody has joined in the game—and he's jumping the highest!

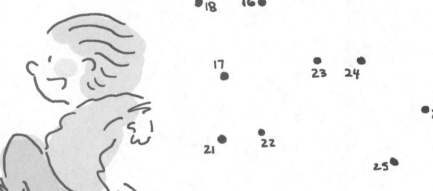
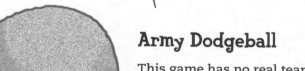

Army Dodgeball

This game has no real teams. Players who are hit in the legs or arms lose the use of that limb. If they are hit on the head or torso, they are out. If they manage to catch a ball thrown by another player, they regain a "missing" limb. The last player standing wins.

Running Home

Baseball is another fast sport that's great fun to play. There's nothing like hitting the ball and racing around the bases to get a home run. Be careful on this puzzle—instead of numbers, you will be connecting letters. Make sure you connect the right A to the right B; there are lots to choose from.

The fastest recorded time circling the bases was set way back in 1932, by Evar Swanson. He hit the ball, ran from first to second to third and made it to home base in 13.3 seconds. It looks like somebody was there to record it, too!

Bouncing Head

Erick Hernández of Cuba holds the record for the most touches of a soccer ball in one minute using only the head: 319. That's a lot of bouncing! It looks like this player has a few more things in the air as well.

HERE'S A GREAT TIP: Let some air out of the soccer ball and it will be a lot easier to control.

5

Splish Splash

Swimming is all about speed. The four main strokes used are freestyle, butterfly, backstroke, and breaststroke. It looks like there are some new members on the team, and they've come up with their own stroke. Can you tell who they are?

What word looks the same upside down and backwards?

It's in the Net

Lacrosse is a great team sport for girls or boys. The object is to catch the ball with a stick that has a net on the end, then run like crazy to get it into the other team's goal. This game gets pretty fast and furious, so be ready to move! It looks like this player has caught something unexpected. How did that get in there?

It is believed that lacrosse was first played by the native peoples of North America. Back then it was a lot different, more like military training than a game. The teams could number in the hundreds (all the way up to 1,000!) and the goals could be separated by many miles.

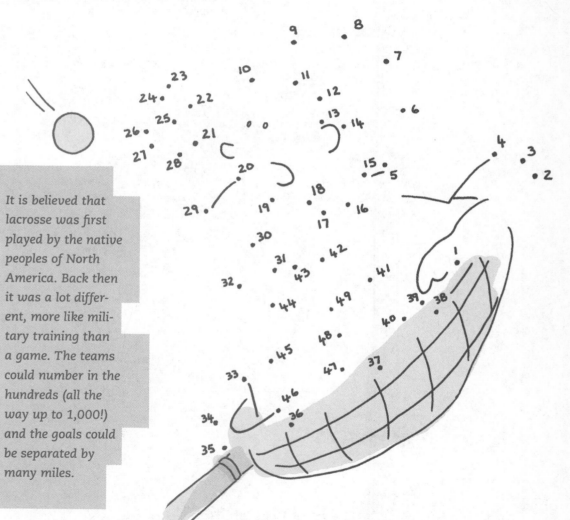

Done To a T Ball

Nobody knows for sure, but experts think T Ball started in the 1940s. Lots of kids learn it before they learn baseball, and because no score is kept, you learn that sports can be fun without having to win. What's happened to this player? He's sure not on the ball—but something else is!

10
9
11
11
8
7
5
6
13
12
15
14
4
3
17
2
18
1

What animal is the best at hitting baseballs? A bat!

Hockey Head

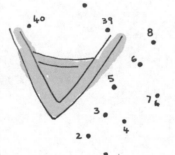
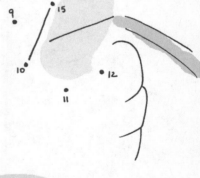

22 •

• 21

23 •

• 20

30

24 • 29 • • 14

• 31 13 •

19 •

28 34
25 • 33 32
21 35
26 42 43 49 36 17
18
48 47
37
44 46 16
41 38
45 9 15
40 39
8
6 12
5 11
7
3 4
2
1

The aim of a hockey game is to get the puck into the other team's net. Because it's usually played on ice, it's one of the fastest games out there. What happened to this player? He didn't keep his eye on the puck!

In hockey, a hat trick isn't a trick you do with your hat—it means you've scored more than one goal. How many do you think it is?

A. 2   B. 3   C. 4

Rowdy Wrestling

One of the first records of wrestling is from China, in 2700 B.C. Things have changed since then—today's wrestlers get nasty! How many wrestlers can you see here?

Here are some holds used in wrestling, along with a few made-up names.
Can you tell which ones are real? See if you can come up with your own names.

Clawhold • **Full Wilson** • **Fujiwara Armbar** • **Eyeball Bulger** •
Triple Turkey Lock • **Double Chickenwing** • **Boston Crab** • **Octopus Hold**
• **Tree of Woe** • **Skin the Cat** • **Snoozing Underarm Takedown**

Spinning Sport

The first basketball net was a beach basket with the bottom still in it, so each time a team scored they had to poke the ball out with a broom. That would sure slow things down! Today, basketball is one of the fastest games out there. It looks like these guys have figured out a way to make the game even faster.

There are lots of tricks you can do with a basketball. In 1999, Michael Kettman of Florida set the record for the most basketballs spun at the same time by one person. He managed to balance and spin twenty-eight basketballs all at once! Amazing!

Why do basketball players love cookies?
Because they can dunk them!

Check that Padding!

In most places in the world, the game we call soccer is called football. To avoid confusion, the rest of the world calls our game American football. Who is this soccer player talking to?

What can you catch
but not throw?
Your breath!

BUT THIS IS
A FOOT BALL !

Because of the injuries in football, players wear a lot of padding. Two other less violent versions were invented. Do you know what they're called?

Slip Sliding Away

If you live somewhere with long, cold winters, skiing is a great sport to learn. Just attach two long, slippery pieces of wood to your feet and throw yourself down the mountain. Wheeee! This skier must be a pro—she's all over the place.

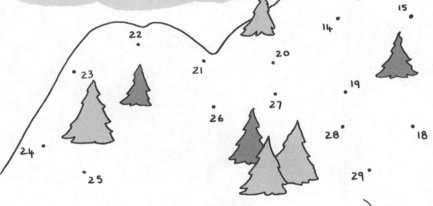

How do skiers stay warm during a competition?

They stay away from the fans.

One of the most unusual water-skiing records was set in 2004 by two blind men. One was the skier, the other the boat driver. They set a blind water-skiing record of 46.2 mph. And to top it off, the skier was seventy-one years old!

Volleybally

Foul! That team has an unfair advantage!

The longest game of volleyball ever played lasted fifty-one hours in Bunbury, Australia, from November 18–20, 2005.

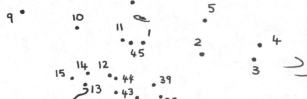
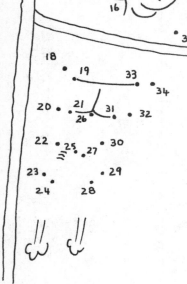

SERVE!

How to serve with a wicked spin:

A. **Stand with your feet slightly apart, one in front of the other.**

B. **While you're looking where you want the ball to go, toss it up in the air—slightly behind your serving shoulder.**

C. **Bend back while you swing your arm back. As you hit the ball, roll your hand over the top. This gives the ball a spin as it hurtles over the net.**

Rex Wrecker

This tyrant lizard looks dangerous. Maybe we'd better warn the dinosaur on the next page that somebody's coming, and he's hungry! Even though we don't know what Tyrannosaurus Rex really liked to eat, it's probably not a good idea to hang around when he's hunting.

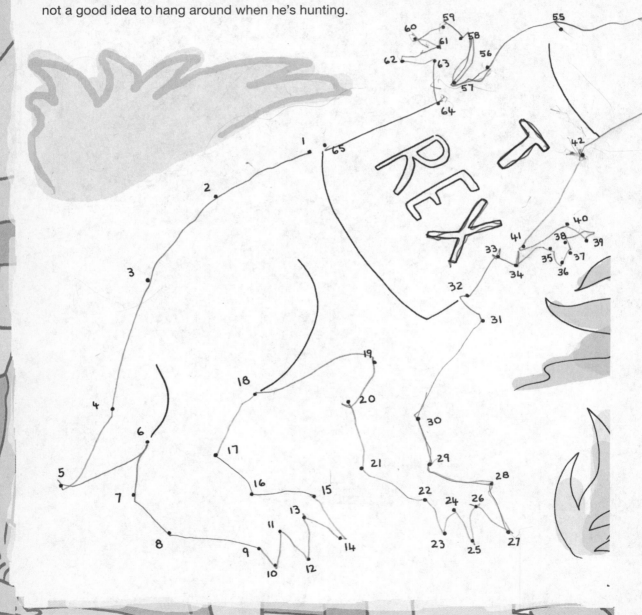

Try and Tri Again

Even though Triceratops could protect herself with her massive horns, she was a plant eater and not believed to be aggressive. Look out, little dinosaur!

What does Triceratops mean?
A. Three-toed claw
B. Three-speed runner
C. Three-horned head

Brutus the Brontosaurus

This dinosaur had a huge body (it could be eighty feet long and weighed in at thirty-five tons) and a tiny head. He must have spent most of his life eating just to stay alive. He was an herbivore, so that's a lot of leaves! Because of the size of his head, scientists believe he wasn't the smartest dinosaur. But just think of the view from up there!

We think of extinction as something rare, but only one in 1,000 species that have ever existed remain today.

Sharpen Up!

C.

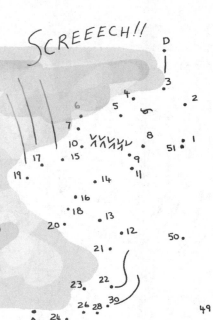

SCREEECH!!

D

The Deinonychus was a terrifying predator, often described as a dinosaur that was built to kill. It was small as dinosaurs go (only five feet tall), but it had sharp teeth in powerful jaws. Each of its three fingers ended in a long, razor-sharp claw. It also had a really big brain, so it probably would have come in at the head of the class.

3

4

6

5

6

2

7

8

10

51

1

17

15

9

19.

11

14

16

18

13

20

12

50

21

23

22

26 28 30

49

B

A

24

25

27

29

31

32

48

46

43

42

47

45

33

44

34

36 38

35

40

37

41

39

There were more than
700 different types of dinosaurs.

19

Mondo Mammoth

The name mammoth comes from the Tatar language and means "earth" (because people used to think mammoths lived underground). The wooly mammoth was no bigger than a modern elephant, but she sure was a lot furrier—that's how she could live in freezing temperatures. Brrrrr! This one sure looks at home.

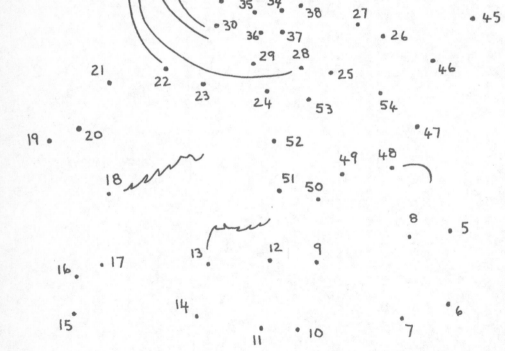

Why wasn't the wooly mammoth allowed to travel on the train?
Because his trunk wouldn't fit in the luggage rack.

Big Baby

When you're a baby animal, you have to know how to hide and stay out of danger. There were plenty of predators that would eat dinosaur babies if they could find the nest they were in. Can you see these baby dinosaurs? They have good camouflage.

How were dinosaurs born? Just like puppies and kittens or more like birds?

Dinosaur Graveyard

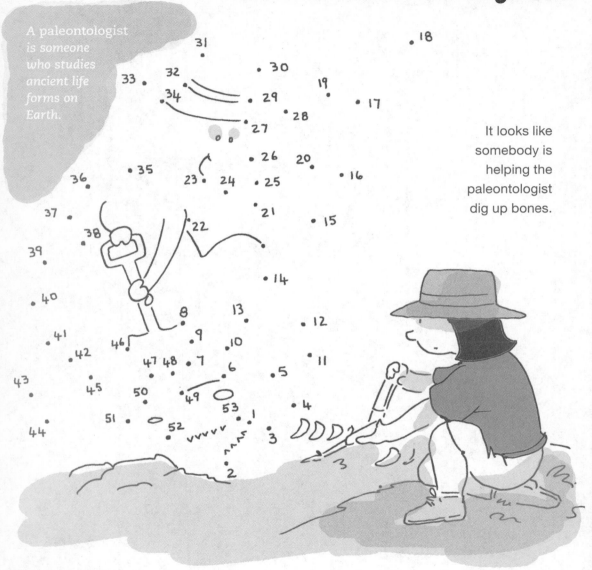

A paleontologist is someone who studies ancient life forms on Earth.

It looks like somebody is helping the paleontologist dig up bones.

A small prairie town in Canada, called Drumheller, is home to the largest collection of dinosaur skeletons in the world. Seventy million years ago it was at the edge of a tropical sea. The dinosaurs died in the mud and sediment, then they were covered with glaciers millions of years later. When the glaciers retreated they scraped away the earth, exposing the dinosaur graveyard.

Digging Dinos

Why did dinosaurs become extinct? That's the biggest question of all, but no one knows for sure. The most accepted theory is that an enormous asteroid crashed into the earth around 65 million years ago. This caused huge changes in the weather and the sun was blocked out, making Earth too cold for the dinosaurs to survive. Hey, it looks like this dinosaur saw something coming.

Dinosaur bones have been found on all seven continents.

23

Dino-tectives

Just like detectives, scientists look for footprints to learn how dinosaurs lived. One hundred and forty million years ago, a dinosaur ran under the hot African sun and left footprints we can still see today. Lucky for us, the prints were undisturbed and the mud turned to stone as millions of years passed. One of these prints wouldn't have been around when dinosaurs roamed the earth. Can you tell which one?

In 1822, Mary Ann Mantell of Sussex, England, became the first person in history to discover something that was recognized as a dinosaur. Earlier discoveries had identified the bones as remains of dragons and other imaginary creatures.

Unclesaurus

Birds and lizards are distant relatives of dinosaurs—like a second cousin twice removed from millions of years ago. Birds and lizards lay eggs and have scaly skin, just like dinosaurs did. Can you see who's in this family picture?

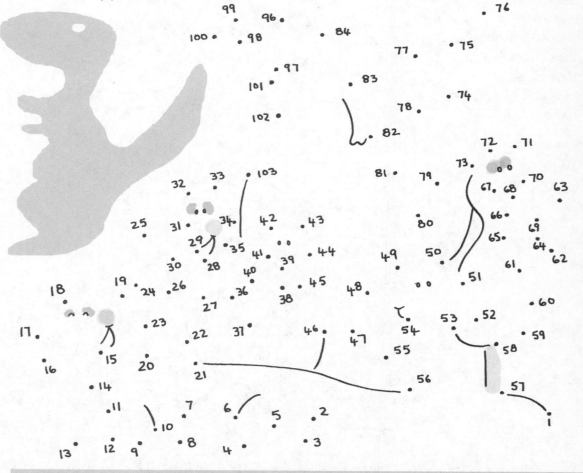

92 91
90
93
86 87 89
94 88
85
95
99 96
100 98 84 76
77 75
97
101 83
102 78 74
82
72 71
73
81 79 67 68 70 63
32 33 103 80 66 69
25 31 34 42 43 49 65 64 62
29 35 50 61
30 28 41 39 44 51
18 19 24 26 40 36 45 48 60
27 38 53 52
17 23 22 31 46 47 54 59
16 15 20 55 58
14 21 56 57
11 7 6 5 2
10 1
13 12 9 8 4 3

The word "dinosaur" was invented by a British scientist named Sir Richard Owen in 1842—it means "terrible lizard."

We know some dinosaurs were very small because tiny dinosaur tracks found in Africa were only two inches long.

Egg-citing

Scientists have discovered fossilized dinosaur eggs. Just like us, dinosaur babies started out walking on all fours until they began to get their balance. Because of their large heads (which make it difficult to move fast), it is also believed the parents would have cared for the babies for some time.

20
16
15
21
19
14
9
17
25 22 13 10
24 23 18
26 28 12 11 8
29
27 7
30 6
5
31 4
32 3
33
34 1 2

I have a little house in which I live all alone. My house has no doors or windows, and if I want to go out I must break through the wall. What am I?

Dino Flight

Did dinosaurs fly? The short answer is no. Even though there were some animals closely related to dinosaurs that flew, they were not actually dinosaurs. Obviously, nobody told this dinosaur!

   Like chickens do today, some dinosaurs swallowed stones to help grind up food in their stomachs.

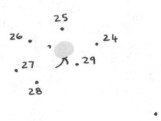

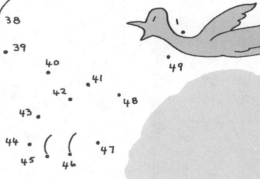

The first dinosaur to be the subject of a song was the *Diplodocus. In the late 1800s, this is what people would sing in pubs in England:*

> *Crowned heads of Europe*
> *All make a royal fuss*
> *Over Uncle Andy*
> *And his old Diplodocus.*

Bird's Eye View

This unsuspecting bird is taking a dangerous flight!

Connect the dots to see where he is going to land if he's not careful.

Some birds really do hang out with crocodiles on the Nile River. They're called Egyptian plovers, but most people call them crocodile birds. Legends say that a crocodile bird will actually fly into the crocodile's mouth to clean the crocodile's teeth. No one has actually proven that this happens, but the birds do pick insects off of the crocodiles' scales.

Chapter 3

BUGS MAGNIFIED

Don't Bug Me!

Ladybugs are also known as the gardener's friend because they eat aphids (aphids eat the gardener's plants). Their bright colors announce to any passing bird, "I taste awful!" But look what happens when you connect the dots on this ladybug—she's sending her own message!

Helping a Lady

Want to give a ladybug a place to live? You can go to a garden supply store and buy ladybug homes that are just like the kind of place they like to hibernate. That way you're helping your own garden and the environment and giving a bug a home!

Speedy Ants

There's a kind of ant that lives in Central and South America that boasts the fastest movement in the animal world. It's called the trap-jaw ant. It can close its jaws at an incredible 145 miles per hour to capture prey. The strike itself only lasts 0.13 milliseconds. That's fast! Who's going to win this race?

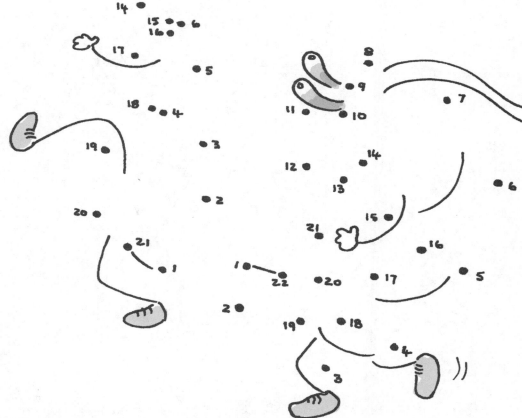

Beetle Bites

Out of 800,000 species of insects on Earth, almost half are different species of beetles. The largest, Titanus giganteus, comes from the tropics and can grow over 6 inches long. He's got a nasty bite, so you don't want to run into him when he's hungry!

The earliest known beetle remains date back about 230 million years, so that means they would have been around the same time as dinosaurs.

How about trying to taste something with your feet? It sounds weird, unless you're a housefly. They have sensory organs in their feet that do just that.

Amazing Feats

MMMMM

Have you ever watched a housefly on your car windshield when you start driving? They can hold on for a long time, even when you're going very fast. That's because they have claws and tiny hairs that hold onto the glass through surface tension.

What's a bug's favorite band?   The Beatles

Planet Plankton

It is some of the smallest life in the oceans and it feeds some of the largest animals, like whales. Plankton floats around in the ocean depending on currents to move it along. In fact, the name plankton means "drifter" in Greek. Where is this plankton drifting?

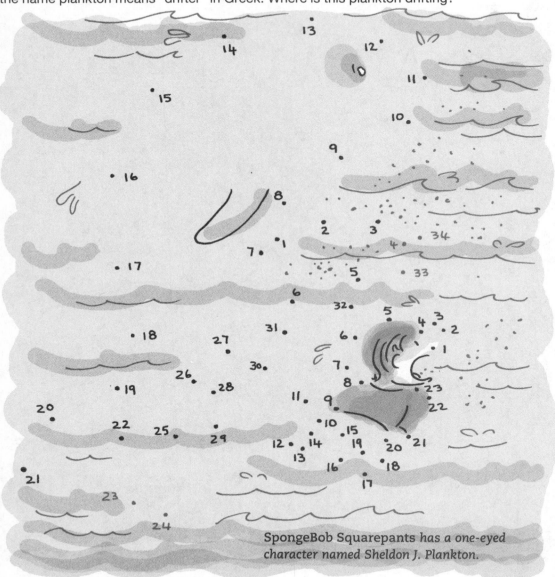

SpongeBob Squarepants *has a one-eyed character named Sheldon J. Plankton.*

Bug Battles

It's a jungle out there, and bugs have developed some truly amazing tricks to survive. There's one group of predators, called mantids, that look just like plants. They wait for their prey to walk by, then jump them. Can you tell which leaf is going to attack?

The giant walking stick insect found in Malaysia and Singapore can grow to an amazing 21.8 inches.

Daring Defense

Because bugs are pretty much at the bottom of the food chain (everyone eats them!), they have to use every trick in the book to protect themselves. Some fight back with sharp fangs, some display bright colors or scary faces, and some taste terrible. Can you tell what defense this bug is using?

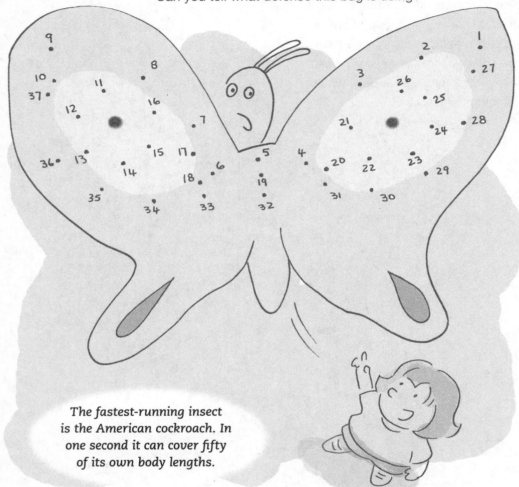

The fastest-running insect is the American cockroach. In one second it can cover fifty of its own body lengths.

Did you hear about the two silkworms that had a race?
— It ended in a tie.

Bug Babies

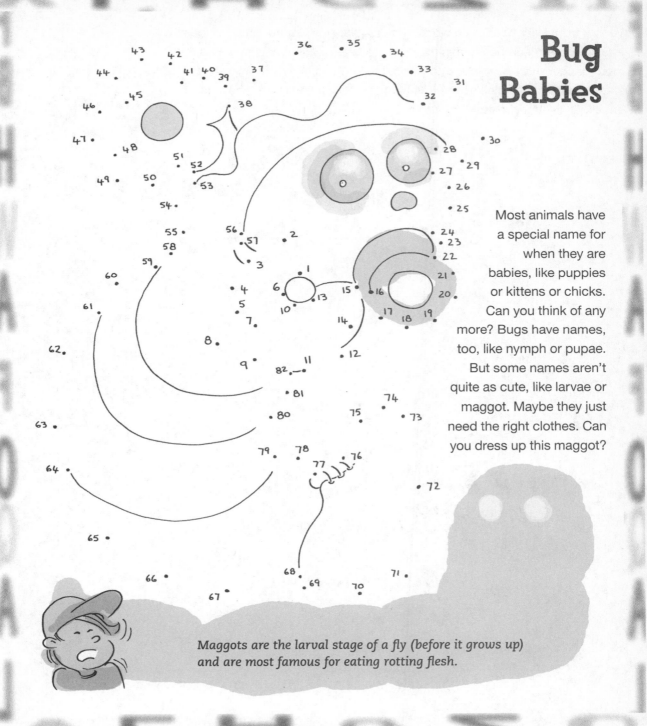

Most animals have a special name for when they are babies, like puppies or kittens or chicks. Can you think of any more? Bugs have names, too, like nymph or pupae. But some names aren't quite as cute, like larvae or maggot. Maybe they just need the right clothes. Can you dress up this maggot?

Maggots are the larval stage of a fly (before it grows up) and are most famous for eating rotting flesh.

Venom from killer bees is no worse than regular bee venom, but killer bees attack in larger numbers when they are provoked, which makes them a lot more dangerous. These bees don't want to sting us (they can only sting once and then they die), so the best thing to do is avoid them. These killer bees look like they're ready to attack!

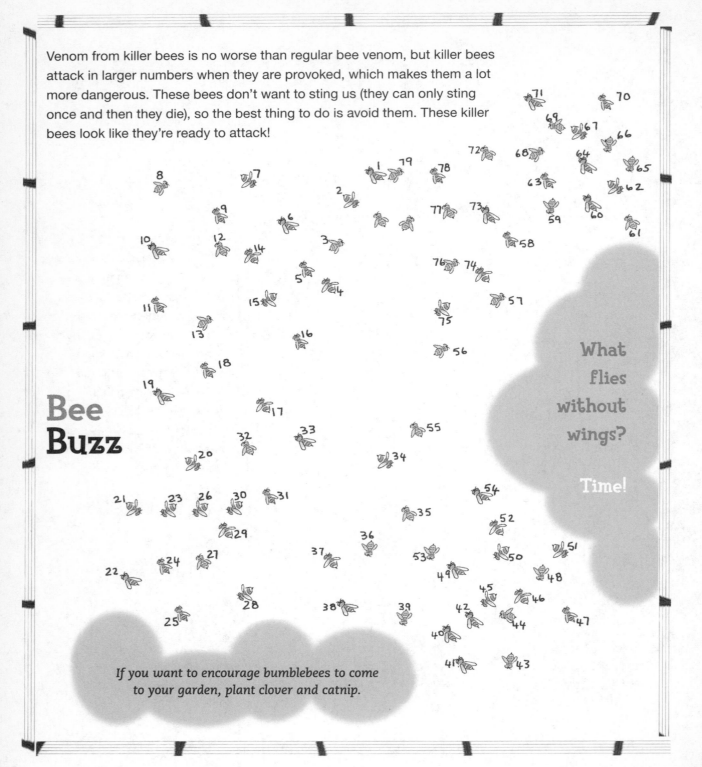

Bee Buzz

What flies without wings?

Time!

If you want to encourage bumblebees to come to your garden, plant clover and catnip.

Flutterby Butterfly

Like all butterflies, the monarch sips food through its proboscis—a long, tube-like tongue. When it's full, it rolls it back up out of the way! There is another butterfly, called the viceroy, which has evolved to look almost exactly like the monarch. Because the monarch is a poisonous butterfly, anything that tries to eat it gets sick. So a lot of predators avoid the viceroy as well. Can you see the difference between these two butterflies?

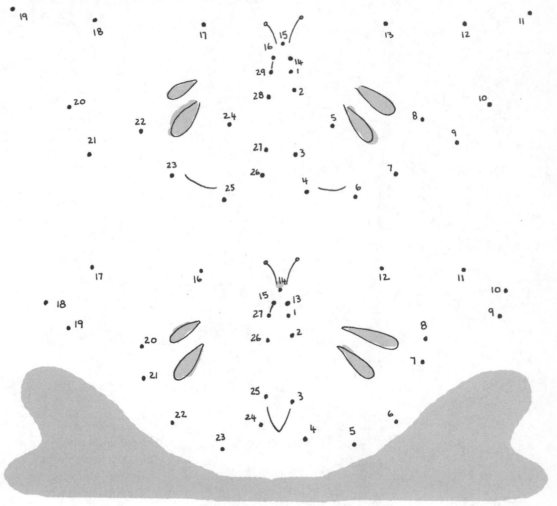

As two caterpillars were crawling along, a butterfly flew overhead. One turned to the other and said, "You'll never get me up in one of those things!"

A stick insect's camouflage is so effective that when it's standing beside a twig it is almost impossible to tell them apart. They are born in a weird way, too. Like a lot of insects, they hatch from eggs, but these eggs can lie on the forest floor for three years waiting for the conditions to be just right to hatch. Even as an egg, they are just like a plant! This stick insect looks like he's not too happy.

Sneaky Stick

Be careful with stick insects. Some species secrete a substance that causes temporary blindness.

Mmmm, Dung!

There are about 400,000 species of dung beetle. When animals leave their droppings, dung beetles eat the nutrients, which are then recycled back into the earth. It's a dirty job, but somebody has to do it! If you ever wondered what a dung beetle sees every day, just connect the dots!

When cows were introduced to Australia, it caused huge problems because the local dung beetles weren't able to handle the giant, wet cowpats. The fields became fouled and fly populations soared to plague proportions. Scientists did research and brought in dung beetles from around the world. The beetles got to work eating and burying the 12 million cowpats produced every hour by Australia's 30 million cows. Problem solved!

It's Not Snot

If you live on the Pacific coast, you might find something strange in your garden. It's ten inches long, bright yellow, and covered in slime. No, it's not a living booger, but what is it?

1. Use the clues to fill in the circles. The last letter of one word is the first letter of the next. Only one letter goes in each circle. When you are done, read the shaded letters in order to learn this slimy critter's name. HINT: It's OK if you seem to be spelling backwards!

2. Connect the dots to get a life-sized portrait of your slippery friend! Use markers or crayons to color him yellow with a few brown spots, just like the familiar fruit it's named after. HINT: Use curving, not straight, lines to connect the dots.

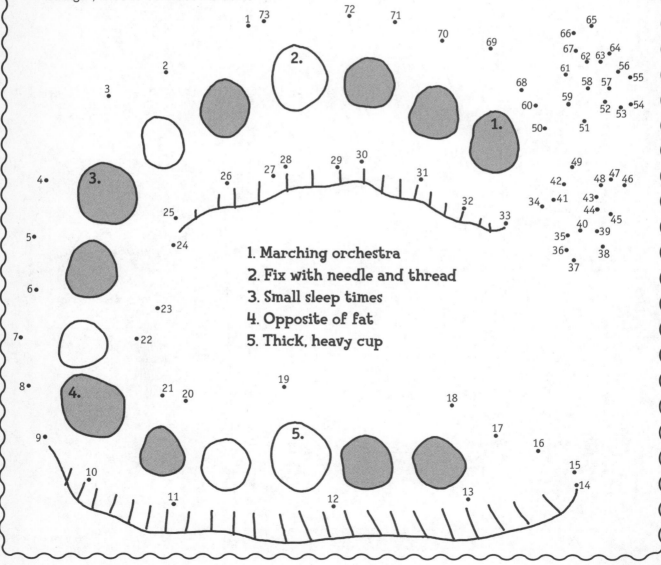

1. Marching orchestra
2. Fix with needle and thread
3. Small sleep times
4. Opposite of fat
5. Thick, heavy cup

Hero Boy + Super Girl

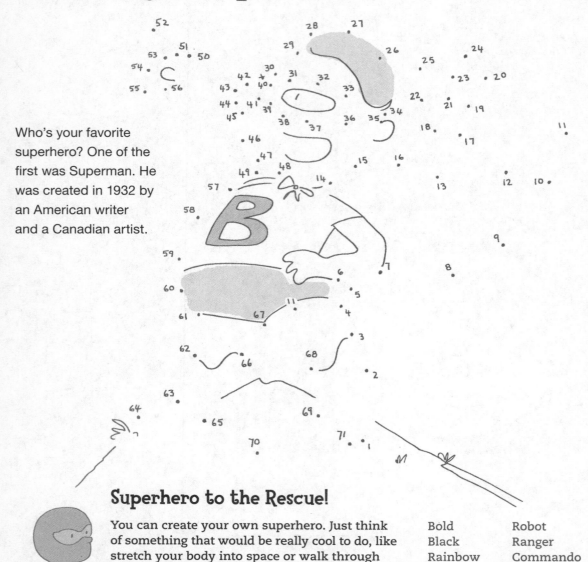

Who's your favorite superhero? One of the first was Superman. He was created in 1932 by an American writer and a Canadian artist.

Superhero to the Rescue!

You can create your own superhero. Just think of something that would be really cool to do, like stretch your body into space or walk through walls. Here are some names to get you started: match the names on the left with the names on the right and, presto, instant superheros!

Bold	Robot
Black	Ranger
Rainbow	Commando
Valiant	Champion
Caped	Defender
Plastic	Power

The Big Escape

Sometimes, spying can be the most exciting job in the world—skiing off cliffs or catching bad guys in disguise. Other times you're just sitting in the dark for hours, watching a boring old door to make sure your suspect doesn't escape. But wait a minute, here's a suspect he probably wasn't expecting!

Spies have been around for thousands of years. Julius Caesar even used them.

Assassi-Ninja

Ninja is the word for spy or assassin in Japanese. They are expert at hand-to-hand combat and concealing their weapons. The bo is a perfect example; it looks like an ordinary bamboo stick, but in the hands of a Ninja, watch out! Or look out for the *shuriken*—throwing stars. They're just flattened pieces of metal with points, but you don't want to get in the way when a Ninja starts throwing them around! How many stars are hidden on this Ninja?

An FBI agent's job is to know as much as she can about criminals. Sometimes you have to be brave and mean. Other times, just being polite can stop a criminal in his tracks. Bank robberies in Seattle dropped by 50 percent after the FBI instructed bank tellers to be overly polite to customers they were unsure of. One suspicious-looking man walked into a bank wearing sunglasses and gardening gloves. When the manager greeted him in a very friendly manner and introduced him to another teller, the would-be robber decided to leave with a simple request for a roll of quarters.

Please and Thank You

The FBI was started in 1908 and was originally called the BOI—Bureau of Investigation.

Go Go Gumshoe

It looks like this detective has walked into a sticky situation.

Another name for a detective is a gumshoe. Nobody knows for sure where the nickname came from, but the most likely explanation is in the list below. Which one do you think it is?

A. They're hard to get rid of because they stick to you like gum.

B. Detectives used to wear soft-soled shoes made of gum rubber.

C. They walked around so much they always ended up with gum on their shoes.

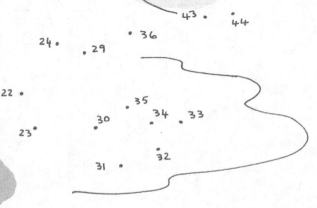

Code Reader

Codes use symbols or letters to represent words or phrases; ciphers replace one letter with another. See if you can decipher this code to see what this detective is doing. You'll have to do a little detective work yourself here; we've replaced the numbers with symbols.

The proper name for people who study codes is a cryptanalyst. Their job is to decipher and create codes. If you want to be a cryptanalyst, it helps if you're good at math and like to figure things out.

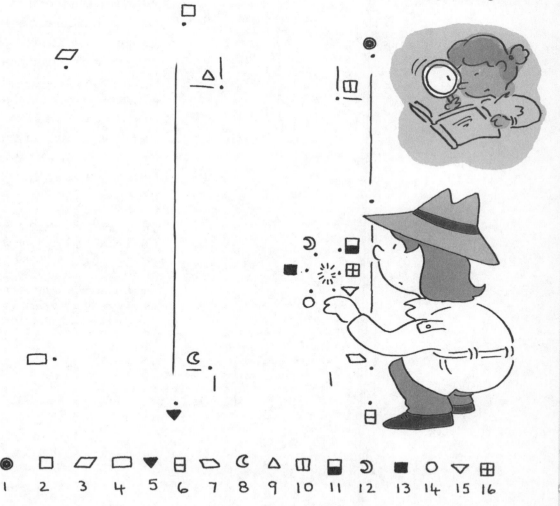

◉	▢	▱	▭	▼	⊟	▱	☾	△	⊞	▢	☽	■	○	▽	⊞
1	2	3	4	5	6	7	8	9	10	11	12	13	14	15	16

And the Award Goes To . . .

When somebody wins an award like an Oscar, it's because a lot of people voted for that person. To make sure the votes are counted properly, a special person called an awards show auditor is hired. He has to be a very honest person so everybody can trust him. This looks like a happy winner.

The winner's name is put in an envelope and given to somebody famous, who opens it and reads the winner's name on stage. Sometimes the accountants even go on stage, just to show there are real people counting votes.

For people who like to shop, this sounds like a fun job, but there is actually a lot of work to do. They don't just go into a store and pretend to shop (or really shop). What they're really doing is finding out how friendly the staff is or how long it takes to get waited on. This girl is trying too hard to convince them she's a shopper!

Mystery shoppers have different names to describe their job. Which one of these do you think is correct?

A. Experience evaluation
B. Mystery customers
C. Spotters
D. Virtual customers
E. Secret shopping

Mystery Shopper

Taster Tester

A food critic has to stay anonymous when she goes to work. If the restaurant knows she is coming, they would cook special food and she would never be able to tell what their food was normally like. This food critic doesn't look too pleased; maybe she forgot to tell the chef she is a vegetarian.

Good food critics are just as good at writing about food as they are at tasting food. And it's good to have a second skill—most food critics don't last more than five years.

Double Danger

Imagine you're a famous actor working on a movie and there's a scene where you need to jump off a cliff and run through a field full of grenades. Your agent thinks it's too risky. That's when you call in the stunt double. They take over when things get too dangerous. This actor looks like he wants a stunt double now!

Animals have stunt doubles, too. Wishbone, the little dog with the big imagination, had a stunt double because he hated to swim.

Abracadabra

These days, magicians use this word when they are doing a trick, but in the second century A.D., it was much more serious. In ancient Rome, if someone had a certain disease, they were told to wear an amulet with the word written as shown.

This lucky charm was believed to ward off the disease and the spirit that brought it.

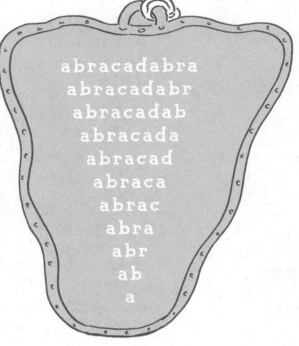

abracadabra
abracadabr
abracadab
abracada
abracad
abraca
abrac
abra
abr
ab
a

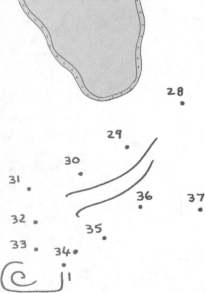

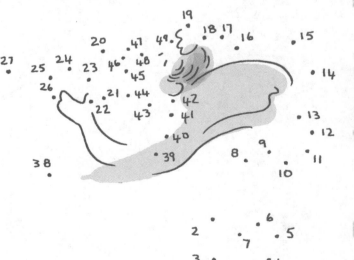

Guard in the Garden

Being a bodyguard requires a lot of skills; it's not just standing around in dark glasses. You have to have a plan of action if somebody attacks the person you're guarding—their life is in your hands! This little star looks very well protected!

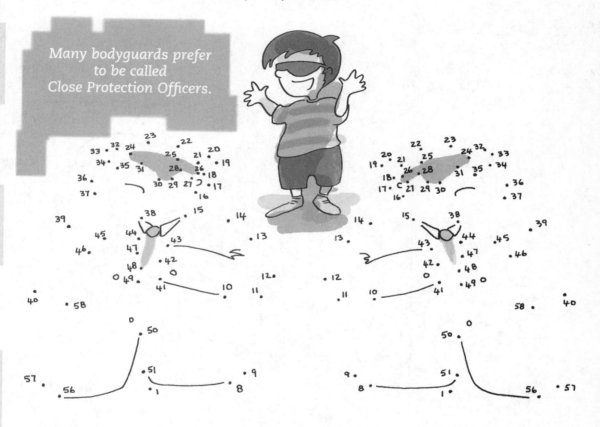

Many bodyguards prefer
to be called
Close Protection Officers.

Ahoy, Me Hearties!

Pirates have been sailing the high seas since ancient times—since the first merchants started using boats to take their cargo from place to place. You can still find pirates roaming the oceans today. They might not look like this guy, and they'll probably have cell phones and speedboats instead of eye patches and peg legs!

Watch Out, Mateys!

There are two sets of dots!
One is numbered 1-85, and the
second set goes from A to Z.

Chapter 5

PIRATES, BANDITS, AND MORE

Mafia Migration

The word mafia comes from an old Arabic word (*mahjas*) meaning "boldness" or "swagger." Originally, the word was used to describe someone who was a bully, but it could also describe someone who was fearless and proud. The Mafia came to the United States from Sicily in the early 1900s. Can you figure out how they arrived here?

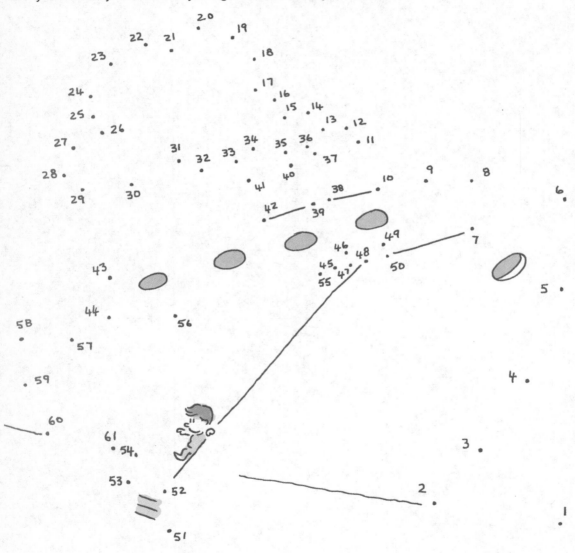

Who's a Yakuza?

Also known as the Japanese Mafia, Yakuza is one of the largest organized crime groups in the world. The word comes from a card game and literally means "good for nothing." Some Yakuza trace their origins to groups that protected the community. They were feared, but they were also occasionally seen as heroes because they protected the town from bandits and gangs. What is this Yakuza taking?

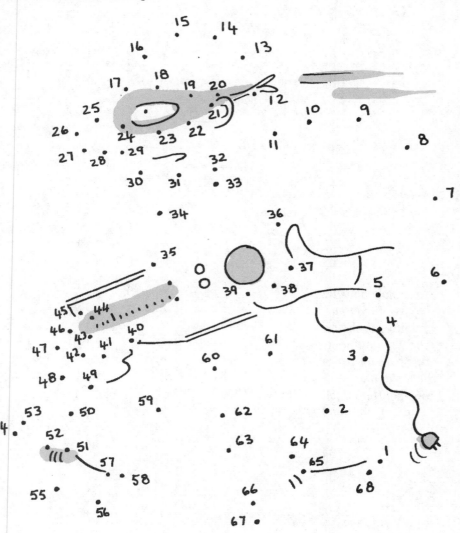

Prison Protest

Believe it or not, prison isn't always for bad people. These two people were thrown in jail after taking part in a protest against nuclear war.

Criminals have lots of free time to get creative. Look at all the different names there are for prison: clink, slammer, pokey, concrete Hilton, joint, and graybar hotel.

Hungry to Escape

Daring escapes are exciting, which explains why there have been so many movies made about them. In one movie, a prisoner kept his soup spoon and turned it into a chisel. He painstakingly carved through a wooden door and made his getaway. It's hard to tell if this prisoner is just hungry or ready to flee.

Why did the robber take a shower? Because he wanted to make a clean getaway.

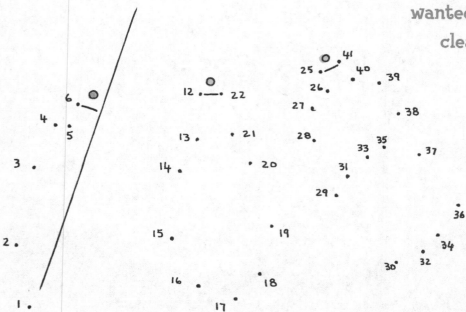

Guessing Gang

Gangs come in all shapes and sizes. Often the name of the gang means they're causing trouble, but it doesn't have to. Sometimes you're just meeting the gang after school for a game of basketball.

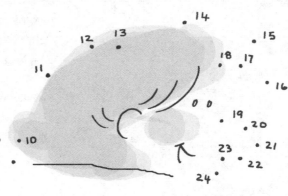

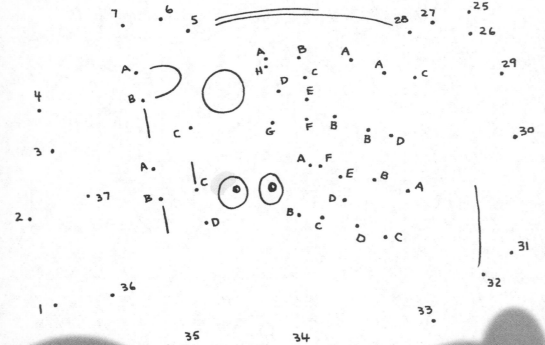

Robin hung out in a gang, but they helped people—at least the poor ones.
They were famous for robbing from the rich and giving to the poor.
Maybe this is what they would be called if they were around today.

Totally Tattoo

Tattoos are popular all around the world, and they go back at least 5,000 years. Just ask Otzi the Ice Man. Well, you can't ask him because he froze to death in the mountains of Europe around 3300 B.C., but he had fifty-seven! Maybe this was one of his tattoos.

Otzi Man, nicknamed Frozen Fritz, was found in a glacier in 1991.

Pricey Pirate

The famous pirate in this puzzle had a couple of distinguishing features—can you connect the dots and find them?

This pirate was created by Robert Louis Stevenson in his novel Treasure Island.

One of the most famous had three words in his name; John was in the middle.

First Name:
A. Short
B. Wild
C. Long

Last name:
A. Bronze
B. Silver
C. Aluminum

Man Overboard!

Mutiny means disobeying the captain of the ship. And when you are at sea, that's pretty scary because there's only one way out—overboard. It looks like this captain is in big trouble.

The remains of the Bounty (a famous ship that was the subject of books and movies) were found at the bottom of the sea near Fiji in 1957.

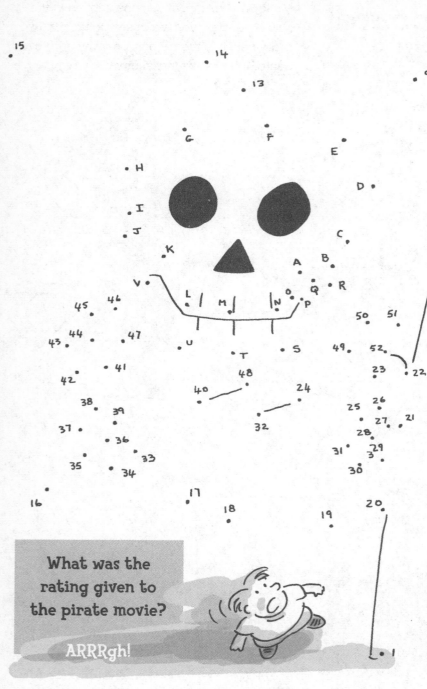

Jolly Roger + Fred + Bill

Pirates are still active today because there is so much traffic at sea—more than there ever used to be. They even use the same flag that was used in the olden days, called the Jolly Roger. Can you tell what it is?

What was the rating given to the pirate movie?

ARRRgh!

Bumbling Burglars

This story is about one dumb criminal and one smart policeman. A woman reporting her car stolen mentioned she had left her cell phone in the car, so the officer quickly called the number. When the thief answered, the officer said he had read the ad in the paper and was interested in buying the car. The thief arranged a meeting and when the officer arrived, he arrested the thief! It looks like there's another bumbling burglar here. Look out below!

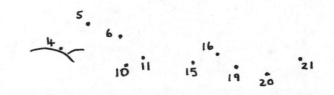

Online Outlaws

Crooks have found a whole new place to practice their crimes. Online fraud is one of the fastest growing areas of criminal activity, so make sure you don't give out any information online that you shouldn't.

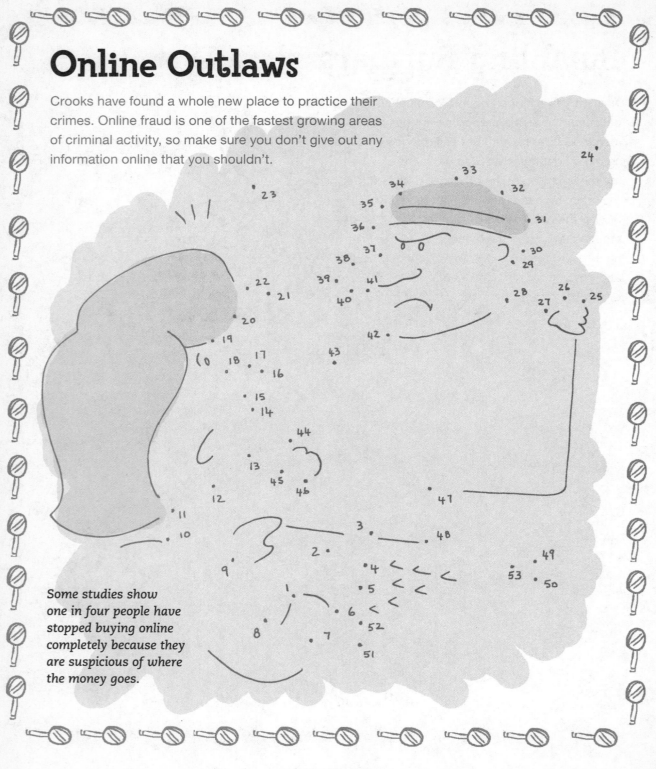

Some studies show one in four people have stopped buying online completely because they are suspicious of where the money goes.

Galloping Princess

This real-life princess is known for all the usual things, like living in a castle and doing charitable work. But she is also known as the only member of the royal family to compete in the Olympics. Do you know who she is?

Hints for a Prince

When a prince chooses a wife, she will very likely become queen, so it's a very big decision. This is the prince who wants to find Cinderella, and he's having a bit of trouble. It looks like he's not sure what a glass slipper really looks like. Can you help him?

What did Cinderella say to
the photographer?
Some day my prints will come.

She's a Queen!

Someone like Queen Elizabeth keeps very busy. She has reigned for more than fifty years, and she has gone on 251 overseas visits to 128 different countries and sat for 120 portraits. This painter can't decide which hat she should wear. Can you see which is right?

The Queen Game

One player is the queen. Other players try to please her by entering the room and offering her something. The queen says "continue" if she's interested, "leave," if she's bored, or "freeze" if she might be interested.

Players who are allowed to continue may approach the queen, and the queen may unfreeze frozen players at her discretion. The game is over when a player is close enough to touch the queen.

The queen can tell a player to leave for any reason: she may not like the message or the way the message is presented. The queen can tell why she does not like the offer: "You know I don't like radishes, so leave!" The queen should be really difficult for the game to be fun. This game is also known as the King Game.

Such a Duchess

A woman who has a title or owns a dukedom (that's an area of land) is known as a duchess. Other times, it just means she is married to a duke. One of the most famous duchesses is a character from Alice in Wonderland, called the Duchess. She must have been very rich—look at her hat!

WHO SAID THIS:
"If everybody minded their own business, the world would go around a great deal faster than it does."

A Duke is one of the highest ranks in British nobility, ranking just beneath a Prince. In England, Prince Philip, the husband of Queen Elizabeth, is also known as the Duke of Edinburgh. Because of the royal connections, the name Duke sounds very fancy and is used for everything from universities to dogs to restaurants. Can you see what the name is for here?

Dashing Duke

The Queen's favorite chef was Knighted Sir Loin.

The Butler Did It!

The word butler comes from the French word *boutellier*, which means cup bearer.

Here are some famous butlers—do you know who works for whom?

___ Alfred Pennyworth
___ Cadbury
___ Jeeves
___ Lurch
___ Rosie the Robot
___ Edgar the Butler

A. Madame Adelaide Bonfamille
B. the Addams family
C. Bertie Wooster
D. Richie Rich
E. Bruce Wayne
F. the Jetson family

Crazy Crowns

The crown jewels are worn by the reigning king or queen. They include things like scepters, swords, orbs, rings, and crowns. How many of these are real kings and queens? You can tell by what they have on their heads.

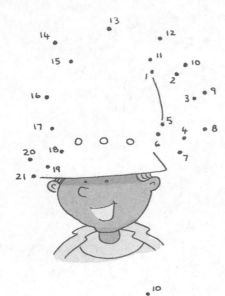

Anne Boleyn, Queen Elizabeth I's mother, had six fingers on one hand.

Living in a castle sounds exciting, but in reality it would have been cold and drafty. The only heat was from the fireplace, and unless you were the king or queen, you probably wouldn't get to enjoy it much. It looks like this servant has found a place to relax while the king and queen are away.

Cozy Castle

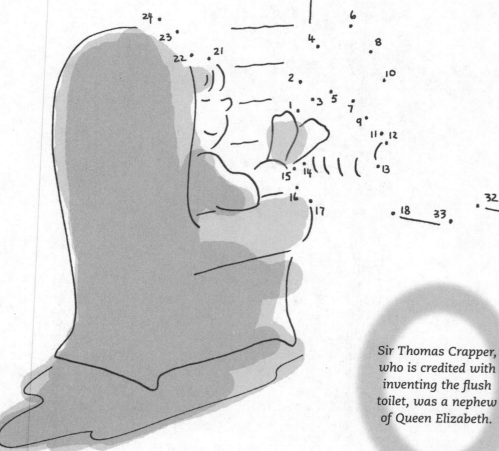

Sir Thomas Crapper, who is credited with inventing the flush toilet, was a nephew of Queen Elizabeth.

This guard is taking care of the tomb of the Unknown Soldier in Arlington, Virginia. Every thirty minutes, twenty-four hours a day, 365 days a year, there is a changing of the guards. Because the requirements are so strict, there have only been 400 soldiers accepted to this position since the tomb was built.

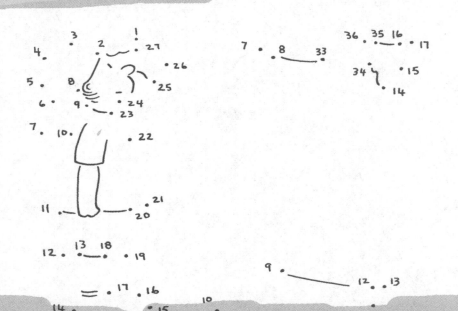

Great Guards

Every guard spends five hours a day preparing himself and his uniform for his turn at guard duty.

Horse House

A stable is a building where livestock, usually horses, are kept. The queen has one for her animals and carriages. It's so big that it also holds many of the cars and vehicles she rides in. Look at this one!

The Gold State Coach is kept in the Royal Mews in England. It is completely covered with gold leaf and weighs four tons. The coach is so heavy that it can only be pulled at a walk by eight horses.

Monarch's Mutts

Queen Elizabeth II loves animals. She rides horses, and she has many dogs to keep her company. Here's an unusual pet the queen was given by the president of Cameroon.

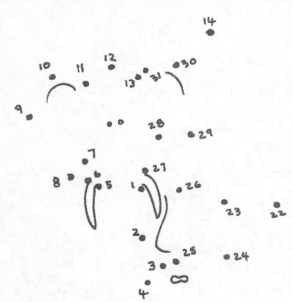

Queen Elizabeth II has owned more than thirty Corgis. She even created a new breed of dog—a mix of Corgi and Dachshund. What do you think this breed is called?

A. Corachshund
B. Corgiund
C. Dorgi
D. Dachshgi
E. Dagi

What is gray and has a tail and a trunk?

A mouse on vacation.

Chapter 7

WHEELS

Vrooom

If you like speed and earsplitting noise, this is the sport for you. Often called the most expensive sport in the world, Formula One racing (involving single-seater cars) can require some teams to spend more than $400 million a year! This one must have cost a lot!

What word is the same spelled forwards and backwards? Here's a hint . . . RA_ _ _ _ _

The first real car race was in France, from Paris to Bordeaux, in 1895.

Pick a Truck

Trucks are used for all kinds of things and come in all sizes.
Can you figure out what kind of truck this is?

garbage • ambulance • fire • street sweeper •
delivery • dump truck • moving van

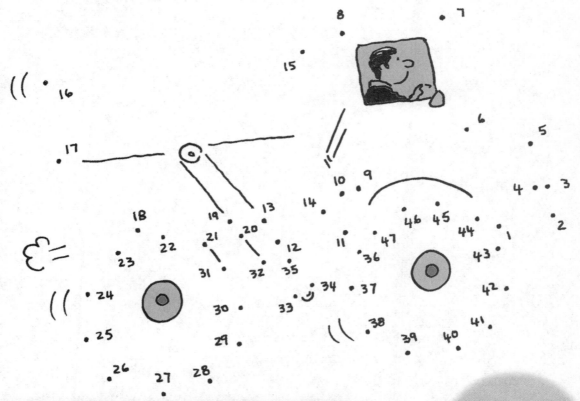

I Spy — Here's a fun activity. Next time you're out in the car, see how many different trucks you can identify—there are lots of them!

We use horsepower to measure the power of an engine. One unit of horsepower can carry 33,000 pounds one foot in one minute.

Amazing Motorcycles

The first motorcycle was powered by steam. People quickly realized that wouldn't work very well, so a clever German invented a motorbike that ran on gas in 1885. There was something very unusual about this bike. What do you think it was?

A. It had sails.
B. It was made of wood.
C. It had to be driven backwards.

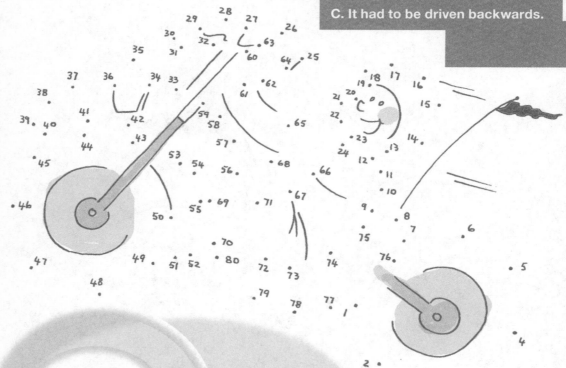

In Athens, Greece, a person's driver's license can be taken away if they appear to be either poorly dressed or unbathed.

Super Model T

The Model T was also known as the people's car, because it was the first automobile that ordinary people could afford. Henry Ford had it constructed on an assembly line to keep costs down. It looks like somebody else wants to go for a ride.

Knock, Knock.
Who's there?
Cargo.
Cargo who?
Car go really fast when you step on the gas.

What a Star!

The sun's rays can be used to fill up a battery so it heats buildings, creates electricity, and moves cars. Even if the sun goes behind a cloud, your car will keep you moving because it stores up energy. I guess we're not the only ones interested in solar power.

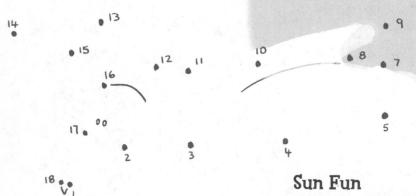

Sun Fun

When the sun (solar energy) hits some colors, it absorbs more energy than others; this means it gets warmer with some colors than others. Here's a fun activity to see if you can predict which color gets warmer.

1. Put three thermometers in the sun.
2. Cover the bulb of the first thermometer with black paper, the second with white paper, and leave the third uncovered.
3. Predict which one will get the hottest.
4. Wait five minutes.
5. Look at the results. Did you predict correctly?

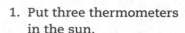

Every minute, enough energy from the sun arrives at the earth to meet our demands for a whole year; we just need to learn how to harness it.

High-Five Hybrid

It's not just cars; San Fransisco is using hybrid buses to help fight global warming. Hybrid just means the engine is using two ways to generate power—most often electricity and gas.

Have you ever seen a hybrid like this before?

Two In One

There are hybrids in the animal world as well. Ever heard of a zeedonk? It's a cross between a zebra and a donkey. It's fun to come up with some names of your own. Here are a few ideas to get you started: What two animals do you think make an elephurkey? A chickelope? Draw the new animals you've created.

The ThrustSSC, a twin turbofan jet-powered automobile, reached 763 mph over a one-mile stretch. Not only is this the fastest land speed ever by a wheeled vehicle, it also broke the sound barrier! To achieve this speed, the car didn't have a regular engine like your family car; it was fitted with jet engines.

Truck Trick

Wheelie, donut, slap wheelie, heart attack, pyramid. What are those things? Monster trucks are not just about racing; these are all terms used to describe different kinds of tricks done by the trucks.

What do you get when you cross an automobile with a household animal?

A carpet!

It's the Biggest!

It's the biggest truck in the world. According to the designer, it's just like driving a house when you climb behind the wheel. But don't expect to see this truck going down your road anytime soon—it's made for mines and quarries. It weighs 400 tons, so much that it would crush regular roads. This is how big you would look if you were standing next to this truck. Wow!

A truck is crossing a bridge one mile long. The bridge can only hold 14,000 pounds, which is the exact weight of the truck. The truck makes it halfway across the bridge and stops. A bird lands on the truck. Does the bridge collapse? Give the reason.

Pedal Power

There are about 1 billion bikes in the world—twice as many as cars. And that's a good thing, since they don't pollute. The first bikes didn't even have pedals—those were added in 1840 by a clever Scottish blacksmith named Kirkpatrick Macmillan.

Another early bike was called a penny farthing. The name comes from the money used at the time in England: the penny and the farthing. The farthing was much bigger than the penny, and when the two coins were laid side by side, they looked just like the bicycle.

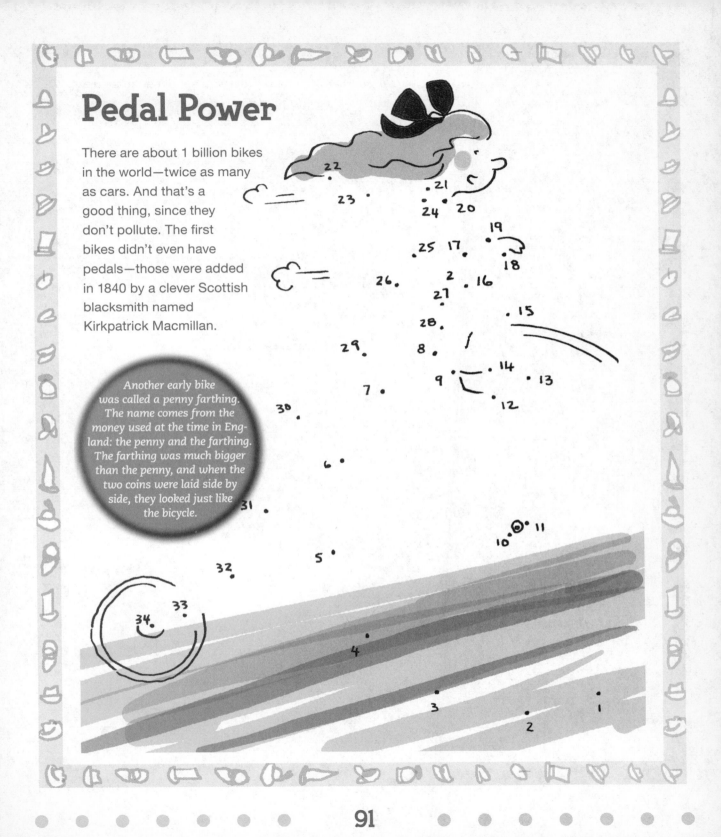

Around the World

Unicycles are very hard to ride at first—you need a good sense of balance. But, just like a regular bike, once you get the hang of it, they're lots of fun. This rider is adding something else.

In different countries, bikes have different names. Can you match the country with the name?

____ Italy
____ Holland
____ Greece
____ United States
____ France
____ Germany

A. Eenweiler
B. Uniciclo
C. Unicycle
D. Monocycle
E. Monopodeloto
F. Einrad

Giddy Up

For many years, the horse and buggy was the main form of transportation in North America. Anybody could drive one—kids would drive them to town or to school. But it looks like one of the passengers here doesn't belong.

In the days when horse and buggy was the main form of transportation, buggies could cost as little as $25 to $50.

Muscle Car

At first, racecars were made for two passengers—the driver and a mechanic. Not only could the mechanic make repairs during a race, he was useful in unexpected ways. In 1912, Ralph DePalma sure needed his mechanic's help to get across the finish line. Connect the dots to find out how these guys managed to stay in eleventh place after their car broke down!

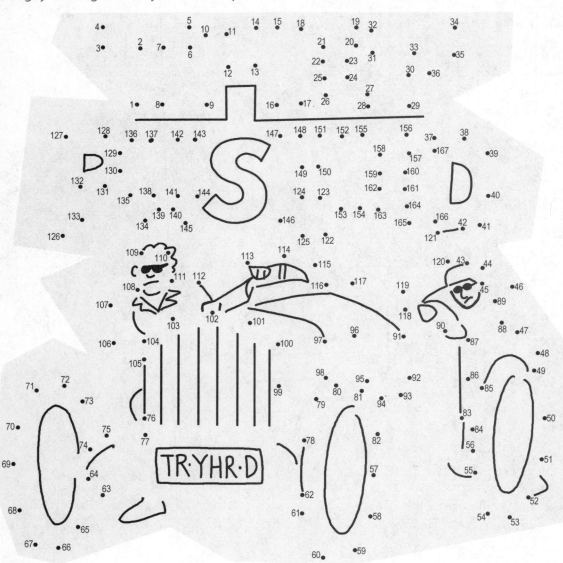

Chapter 8

PETS AND ANIMALS

Ancient Pussycat

You can tell from the way this cat's tail is twitching he doesn't know which way to go. I wonder what he sees.

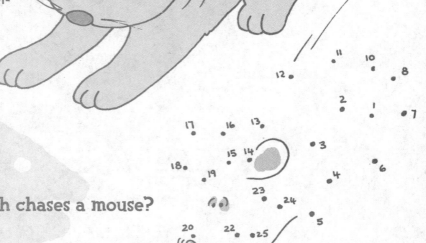

Scientists recently discovered a grave with a cat and a human in it, showing we've kept cats much longer than previously thought. How long do you think we've had pet cats?

A. 2,000 years
B. 4,000 years
C. 7,500 years
D. 9,500 years

What kind of fish chases a mouse?
A catfish!

Dog Tails

Dogs are part of the family that includes wolves, coyotes, and foxes. Archeologists think domesticated dogs (like your pet Poodle) came from wolves that entered our settlements looking for food about 12,000 years ago. Next time Fluffy is at the table looking for scraps, think of that. Today, dogs look different than they did back then. Can you see how this owner has dressed her dog?

What goes tick-tick, woof-woof?
A watch dog.

Dastardly Dragons

In mythology, dragons live up to 1,200 years. They are also believed to have a huge store of knowledge and treasure, like gold and rubies. When you think of it, it all makes sense: Imagine having that long to gather all that stuff! It looks like this dragon is still trying to learn more. Can you see what he is doing?

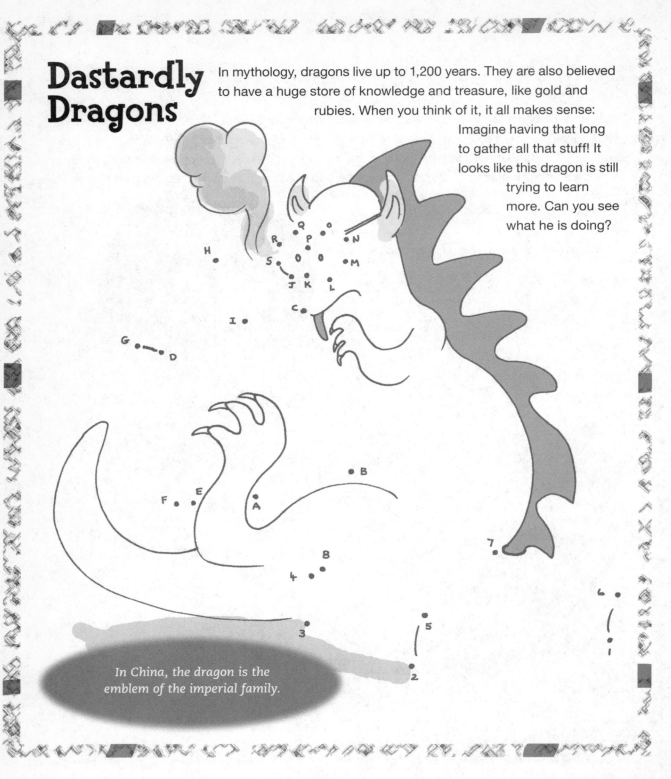

In China, the dragon is the emblem of the imperial family.

Unique Unicorns

A unicorn is a beautiful mythical creature. According to legend, it has white hair and a long horn in the middle of its head, which is believed to be able to heal wounds. Here's another kind of make-believe unicorn.

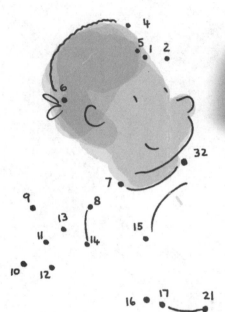

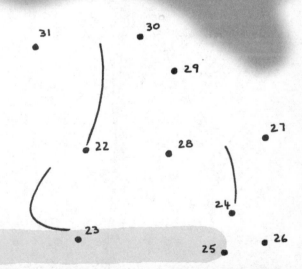

You as a Unicorn

Make your own unicorn horn. When you're finished with a roll of aluminum foil or food wrap, save the cardboard tube and punch two holes at one end. Thread a string through the two holes, then tie it around your head.

The word unicorn comes from Latin. What do you think it means?

A. one-horned   B. white mane   C. unique horse

Chatty Zebra

Each species of zebra has its own unique stripes. The further south you travel in Africa, the further apart the stripes get. This zebra looks like he's trying to send us a message. Can you see what he's trying to say? Join A to B like normal, but watch out—there are lots of As and Bs, so which one connects to which?

If a dictionary goes from A to Z,
what goes from Z to A?

A zebra.

Incoming Frog

Some frogs in captivity have lived forty years. This dragonfly looks like he's in danger; can you see what's coming?

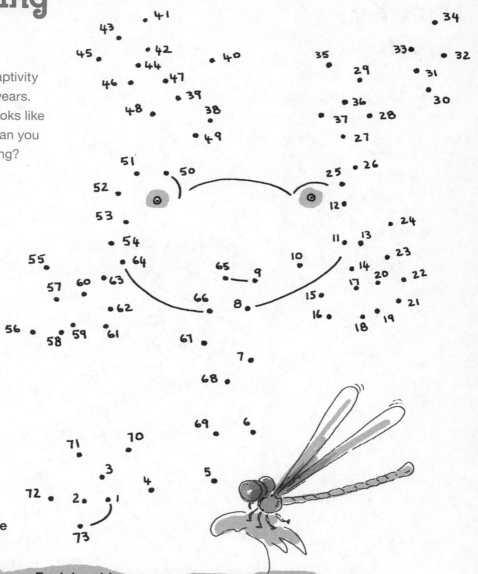

Which one of these is not a real frog?

A. bullfrog
B. green frog
C. leopard frog
D. marsh frog
E. pickerel frog
F. lump frog
G. wood frog?

What do you call a group of frogs?

A. army
B. herd
C. school
D. flock

Sneaky Snakes

Snakes can swallow prey three times their own size. There have been recorded cases of snakes swallowing tigers. That's a big dinner! Most people believe that if you put a snake in a small cage it will stop growing, but this is not true. Snakes continue to grow no matter where they are. This snake must have been very hungry.

Why can't you play a joke on a snake?

Because you can never pull his leg.

Shark Show

Modern studies have shown sharks are not the evil monsters they have been portrayed to be. Sharks have been hunted so relentlessly that now some species are endangered. The gentle giant known as the basking shark only eats plankton. The great white is the only shark known to lift its head above the water to look at objects on the surface. It looks like this photographer has found a friendly one. What kind of shark is this?

Eagle Eyes

The bald eagle isn't really bald at all. It is believed the word comes from the old English "balde," meaning "white." We're lucky to have it as our national bird: It is said Benjamin Franklin didn't like the choice of the eagle as a national emblem— he wanted a turkey.

What grows up while growing down?

A goose.

Ride 'Em Cowboy!

More than 400 years ago, Spanish explorers brought horses to North America. Today, descendents of these horses still roam free—they are called mustangs.

Mustang

Here's a fun game. How many other words can you find in within the word mustang? The words have to be at least three letters long. We found eight, but there's more if you really look.

What is a horse's favorite sport?

Stable tennis.

Jumpy Giraffes

Giraffes have many different ways to defend themselves. One way is to kick with their hooves (they can kill a lion). Other times, they neck wrestle with other giraffes. This one looks a bit confused— who is he wrestling with?

Here's a fun thing to do— have you ever measured your own tongue? A giraffe's tongue can grow up to eighteen inches long! How do you measure up?

Chapter 9

GROSS!

Ickety Crickety

Crickets are known for their chirping noise, but in some cultures they make a tasty dessert! What if things were the other way around?

Why don't grasshoppers go to baseball games?

They prefer cricket.

Boogers Away!

What do you think is the best way to clear out your nose? Picking your nose isn't so good because there are tons of germs; the best way is to blow with a tissue. When you have a nose like this, you need a lot of tissues!

Guess how much snot you produce every single day?

A. 1 teaspoon
B. ½ cup
C. 1 cup
D. 1 gallon

What's the difference between broccoli and a booger?
Kids don't eat broccoli!

On the other side of the ocean, they call them bogeys.

What did the leg bone say to the foot?

Stick with me and you'll go places.

It Came from Inside

It's pretty hard to do, but bones can break if you go flying off your bike or skateboard. They can be anything from a major break that sticks right through the skin (ouch!) to a fracture that doesn't hurt at all. This daredevil has probably had a few broken bones.

Mmmm, Slime

Slugs often follow their slime trail back to where they had their last meal if it was really good.

Slugs are covered in slime, and they love it. It protects them from drying out and allows them to slide along the ground more easily. This slug looks like she's having fun!

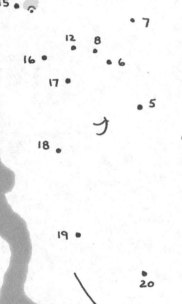

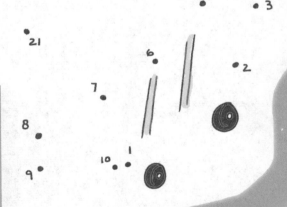

A sloth is out for a walk when he's mugged by four snails. After recovering his wits, he goes to make a police report. "Can you describe the snails?" asks the officer. "Not well. It all happened so fast," replies the sloth.

Stinkorama

Scientists in America are working on developing the world's worst smell. It will be used for crowd control when it is done. It has been difficult to do because a lot of what we react to is based on our own individual memories. It looks like this animal is making a lasting impression.

43
41   40
44   38
42   39   37
36
45
35
46
34
47
48
33
49
50
32
51
6   52   2   31
4   30
5   3   1
7
8   24
9   0'   23   25   29
10   12   17   22   26   28
11   U   16   18   21   27
13   20
15
14   19

Which one of these is the smell you hate the most?

toilet • bad breath • fish •
Brussels sprouts • burps • vomit
• running shoes • car exhaust

See if you can think of five more.

Worm World

Our world would be pretty boring if it wasn't for worms. They increase the amount of air and water in the soil, and they break down things like leaves and grass so plants can grow. After worms eat, they leave behind their own fertilizer. When it rains too much, worms have to come up for air. It looks like these guys came prepared.

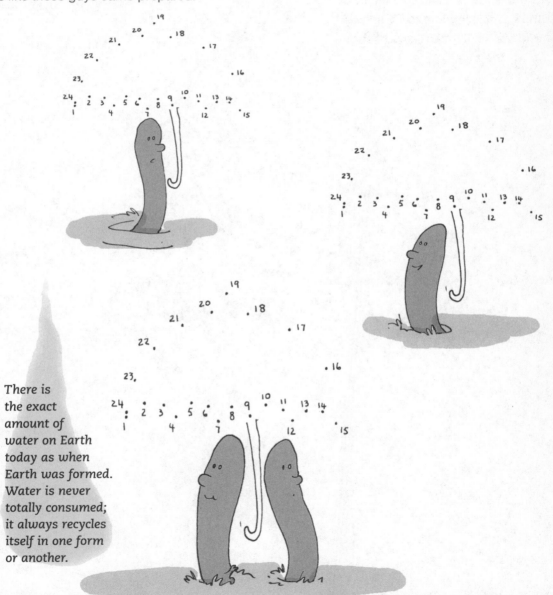

There is the exact amount of water on Earth today as when Earth was formed. Water is never totally consumed; it always recycles itself in one form or another.

Slime Surprise

Slime is found all around us, from the animal kingdom to TV shows and books. It looks like somebody made too much slime!

Presto Scabo

You've probably had one. One minute you're running along, the next you've tripped and suddenly you have a big cut. But the blood that's rushing through your veins also carries tools to heal you. There are little things called platelets and fibrin that build a natural band-aid, also called a scab. Let the healing begin!

This soccer player better watch out or he'll be getting his own scab soon!

Dirty
Digits

Dirt that ends up on your toes is made up of four things: stones, sand, clay, and humus. Humus is the ickiest part—it's made up of dead plants and animals that are slowly being eaten by bugs and bacteria. Just imagine all that activity between your toes if you don't wash your feet! Eeeyeww!

What's the stink under the sink? If you have leaky pipes under your sink, there's a good chance you have mold. Mold loves to grow anywhere it's dark and damp, and some types can be dangerous to breathe. But don't worry too much—molds, fungus, and spores are in the air we breathe every day, and 99.9 percent of them are not harmful. This family needs to clean more!

Under the Sink

The best way to make sure you don't get mold is to remember the letters C, D, and V—keep areas Clean, Dry, and Ventilated.

Kiss the Dog

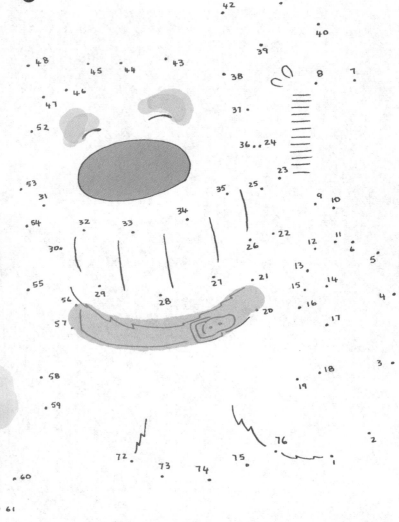

Is a dog's mouth really cleaner than a human's? Yes and no. A dog has just as many germs in its mouth, but dog germs tend to cause problems for other dogs, not humans. Your dog should have her teeth brushed every day with her own special pet toothbrush and toothpaste. Toothpaste for dogs comes in flavors like chicken and liver. It looks like somebody has figured how to do it on her own!

CHAPTER 1: SPORTS AND GAMES

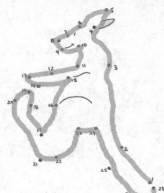

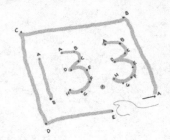

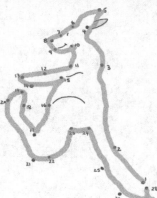

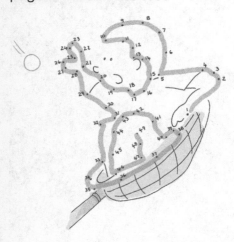

SWIMS looks the same upside down and backwards.

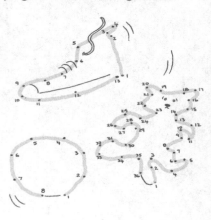

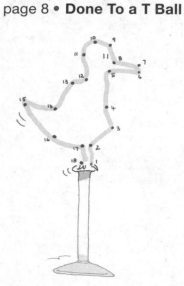

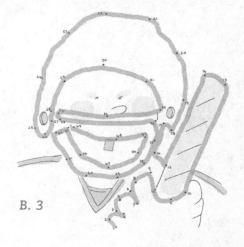

B. 3

PUZZLE ANSWERS

page 10 • Rowdy Wrestling

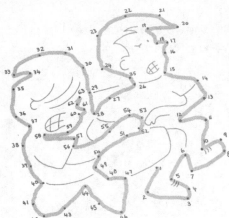

These are real wrestling holds: Clawhold, Fujiwara Armbar, Double Chickenwing, Boston Crab, Octopus Hold

page 11 • Spinning Sport

page 12 • Check that Padding!

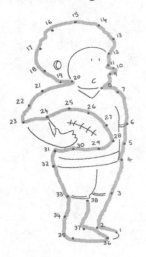

page 13 • Slip Sliding Away

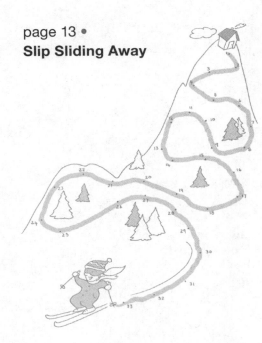

page 14 • Volleybally

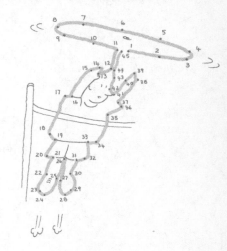

Flag football and touch football are two less violent versions of full contact football.

CHAPTER 2: AS BIG AS A DINOSAUR

page 16 • **Rex Wrecker**   page 17 • **Try and Tri Again**

page 18 • **Brutus the Brontosaurus**

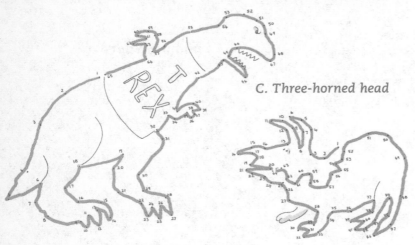

C. Three-horned head

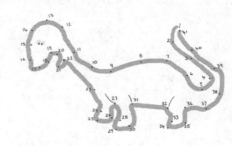

page 20 • **Mondo Mammoth**

page 19 • **Sharpen Up!**

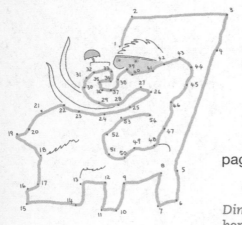

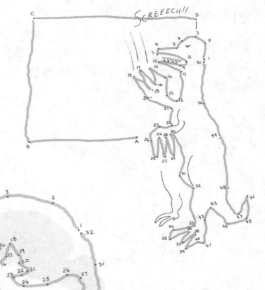

page 21 • **Big Baby**

Dinosaurs were born in eggs, just like birds and lizards.

PUZZLE ANSWERS

page 22 • Dinosaur Graveyard

page 23 • Digging Dinos

page 24 • Dino-tectives

page 26 • Egg-citing

An egg.

page 25 • Unclesaurus

There are two lizards, three birds, and a dinosaur.

page 27 • Dino Flight

page 28 • Bird's Eye View

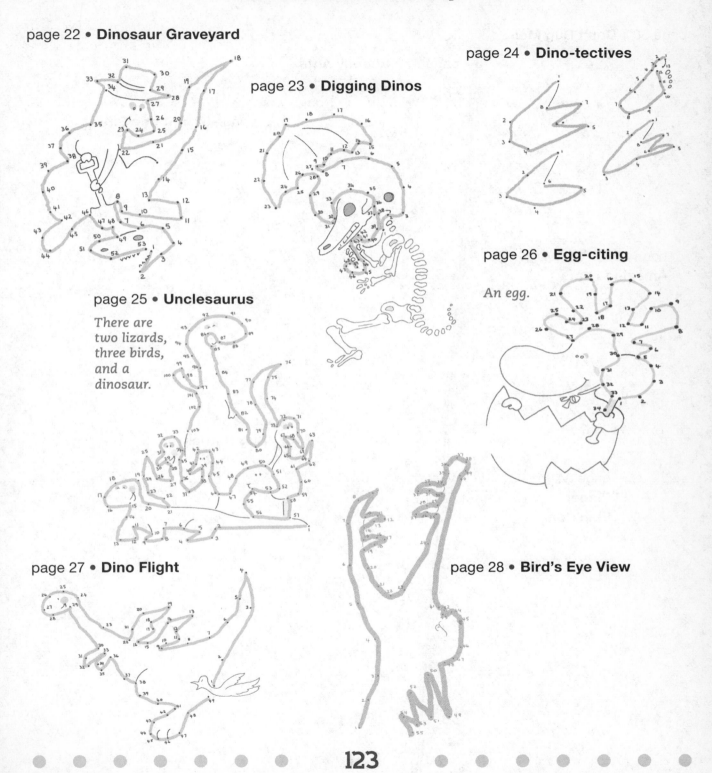

CHAPTER 3: BUGS MAGNIFIED

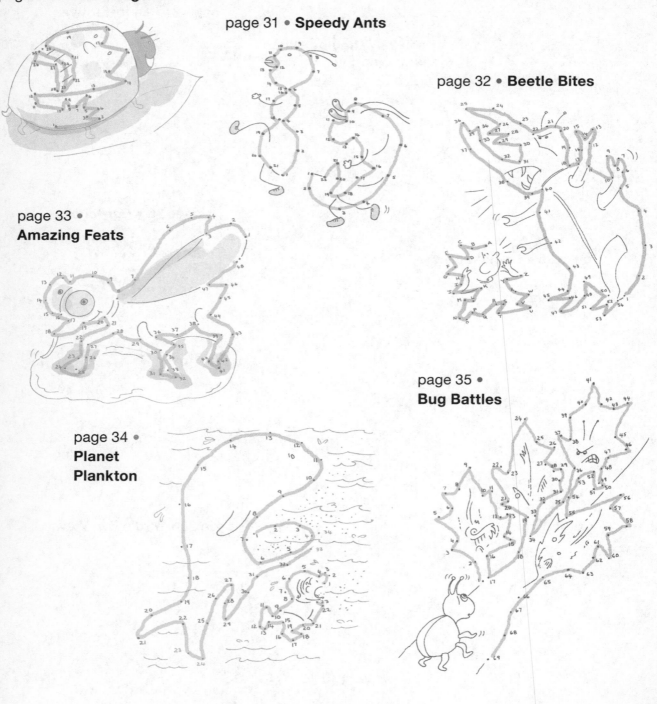

PUZZLE ANSWERS

page 36 • **Daring Defense**

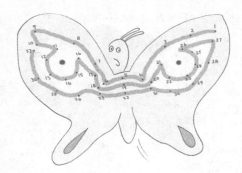

page 37 • **Bug Babies**

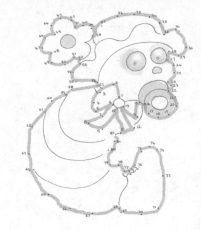

page 38 • **Bee Buzz**

page 39 • **Flutterby Butterfly**

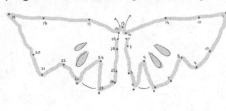

page 41 • **Mmmm, Dung!**

page 40 • **Sneaky Stick**

I AM AN INSECT NOT A STICK!

page 42 • **It's Not Snot**

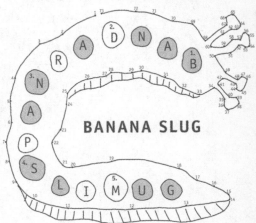

BANANA SLUG

CHAPTER 4: SECRET JOBS

page 44 • **Hero Boy+Super Girl**

page 45 • **The Big Escape**

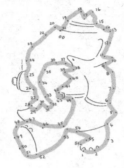

page 46 • **Assassi-Ninja**

There are two stars hidden in the Ninja.

page 47 • **Please and Thank You**

page 48 • **Go Go Gumshoe**

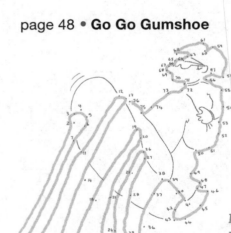

B. Detectives used to wear soft-soled shoes made of gum rubber.

PUZZLE ANSWERS

page 49 • **Code Reader**

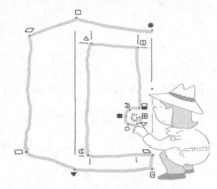

page 50 • **And the Award Goes To . . .**

page 51 • **Mystery Shopper**

They're all correct names for a mystery shopper.

page 52 • **Taster Tester**

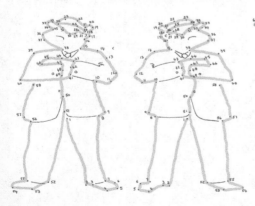

page 53 • **Double Danger**

page 54 • **Abracadabra**

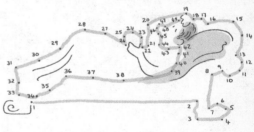

page 55 • **Guard in the Garden**

page 56 • **Ahoy, Me Hearties!**

CHAPTER 5: PIRATES, BANDITS, AND MORE

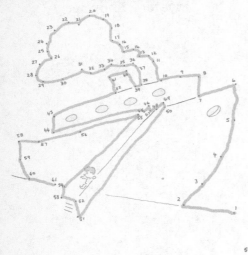

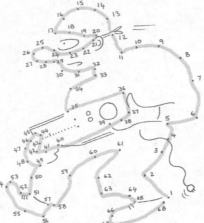

PUZZLE ANSWERS

page 64 • Pricey Pirate

The famous pirate's name was Long John Silver.

page 65 • Man Overboard!

page 66 • Jolly Roger + Fred + Bill

page 67 • Bumbling Burglars

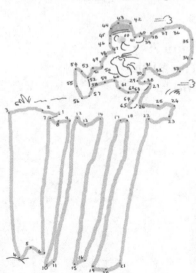

page 68 • Online Outlaws

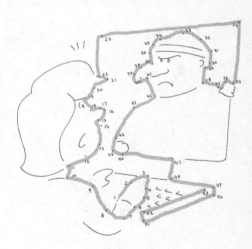

CHAPTER 6: IT'S A ROYAL LIFE

page 70 • **Galloping Princess**

page 71 • **Hints for a Prince**

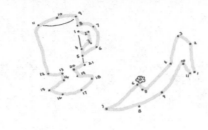

page 72 • **She's a Queen!**

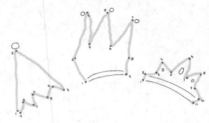

Britain's Princess Anne competed on horseback in the 1976 Olympics.

page 74 •
Dashing Duke

page 73 • **Such a Duchess**

The Duchess from Alice in Wonderland.

page 75 •
The Butler Did It!

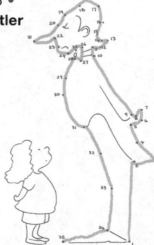

Alfred Pennyworth—Bruce Wayne's butler in Batman

Cadbury—the Rich family's butler in the Richie Rich comic book series

Jeeves—Bertie Wooster's butler in P. G. Wodehouse's books

Lurch—the Addams family's butler in The Addams Family

Rosie the Robot—the Jetson family's maid in The Jetsons

Edgar the Butler—Madame Adelaide Bonfamille's butler in the Aristocats

PUZZLE ANSWERS

page 76 • **Crazy Crowns**

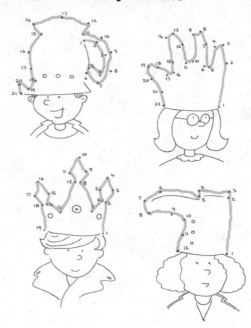

page 77 • **Cozy Castle**

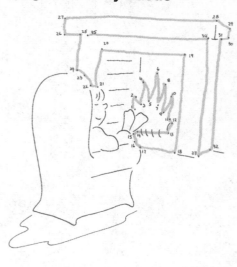

page 78 • **Great Guards**

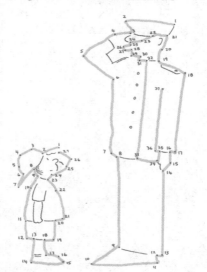

page 79 • **Horse House**

page 80 • **Monarch's Mutts**

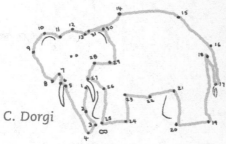

C. Dorgi

CHAPTER 7: WHEELS

page 82 • Vrooom

Racecar is the same spelled forwards and backwards.

page 83 • Pick a Truck

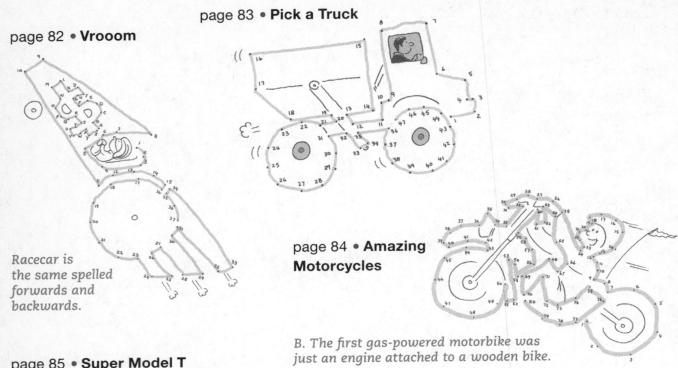

page 84 • Amazing Motorcycles

B. The first gas-powered motorbike was just an engine attached to a wooden bike.

page 85 • Super Model T

page 86 • What a Star!

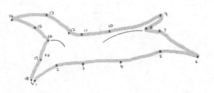

page 87 • High-Five Hybrid

PUZZLE ANSWERS

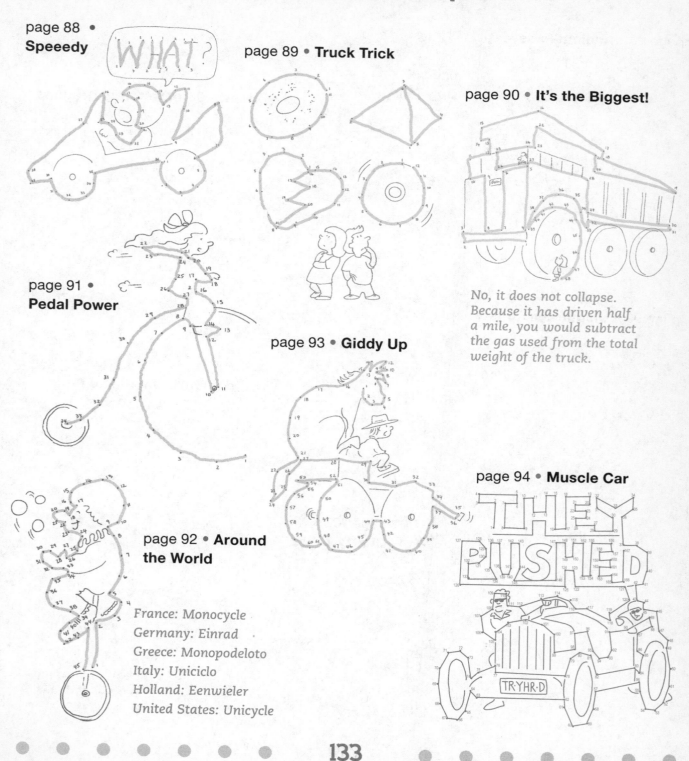

page 88 • **Speeedy**

page 89 • **Truck Trick**

page 90 • **It's the Biggest!**

No, it does not collapse. Because it has driven half a mile, you would subtract the gas used from the total weight of the truck.

page 91 • **Pedal Power**

page 93 • **Giddy Up**

page 94 • **Muscle Car**

page 92 • **Around the World**

France: Monocycle
Germany: Einrad
Greece: Monopodeloto
Italy: Uniciclo
Holland: Eenwieler
United States: Unicycle

CHAPTER 8: PETS AND ANIMALS

page 96 • **Ancient Pussycat**

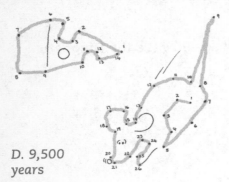

D. 9,500
years

page 97 •
Dog Tails

page 98 • **Dastardly Dragons**

page 99 • **Unique Unicorns**

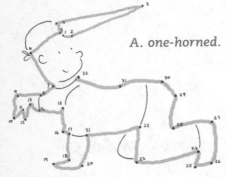

A. one-horned.

page 101 • **Incoming Frog**

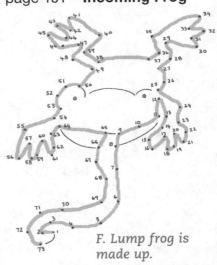

page 100 •
Chatty Zebra

F. Lump frog is
made up.

A. A group of frogs
is called an army.
A group of toads is
called a knot.

PUZZLE ANSWERS

page 102 • Sneaky Snakes

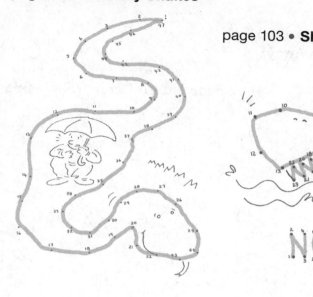

page 103 • Shark Show

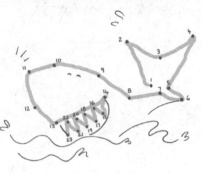

page 104 • Eagle Eyes

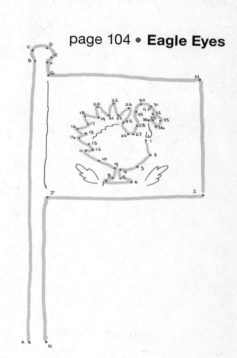

page 105 • Ride 'Em Cowboy!

Mug
Sun
Gun
Stag
Gnat
Mast
Stun
Must

**page 106 •
Jumpy Giraffes**

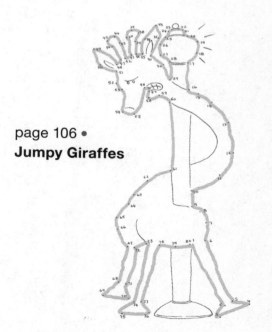

CHAPTER 9: GROSS!

page 108 • **Ickety Crickety**

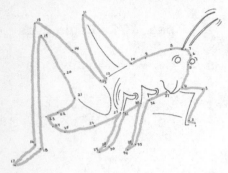

page 109 • **Boogers Away!**

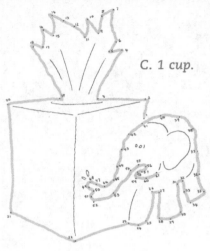

C. 1 cup.

page 110 • **It Came from Inside**

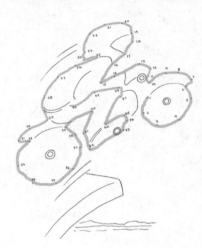

page 111 • **Mmmm, Slime**

page 112 • **Stinkorama**

page 113 • **Worm World**

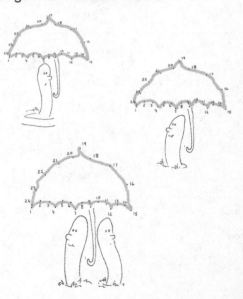

PUZZLE ANSWERS

page 114 •
Slime Surprise

page 115 •
Presto Scabo

page 116 • **Dirty Digits**

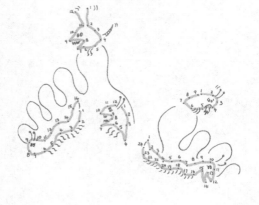

page 117 •
Under the Sink

page 118 •
Kiss the Dog

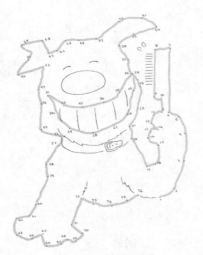